ESSENTIAL DK COMPUTERS

INTERNET

BUILDING
A WEBSITE

ABOUT THIS BOOK

Building A Website is an easy-to-follow guide to Microsoft's Website building program, FrontPage 2000. This book is for anyone who has little or no experience with FrontPage 2000.

FRONTPAGE 2000'S FEATURES, FROM creating a new site to publishing it on the Web, are presented in separate chapters to allow easy understanding of their functions and how to carry them out.

Within each chapter, you'll find subsections that deal with self-contained procedures. These build on previous explanations, so your knowledge can be gradually developed through a logical sequence of actions.

The chapters and the subsections use a step-by-step approach. Almost every step is accompanied by an illustration showing how your screen should look. The screen images are either full-screen or they focus on an important detail that you'll see on your own screen. If you work through the steps, you'll soon start feeling comfortable that you're learning and making progress.

The book has several features to help you understand what is happening and what you need to do. A labeled FrontPage 2000

window is included to show you where to find the important elements in this program. This is followed by an illustration of the rows of buttons, or "toolbars," at the top of the screen, to help you find your way around these invaluable, but initially perplexing, controls.

Command keys, such as ENTER and BACKSPACE, are shown in these rectangles: Enter↵ and ← Bksp, so that there's no confusion over what keys should be pressed. Cross-references are shown in the text as left- or right-hand page icons: ◄ and ►. The page number and the reference are shown at the foot of the page.

There are also boxes that explain a feature in detail, and tip boxes that provide alternative methods and shortcuts. Finally, at the back, you'll find a glossary explaining new terms and a comprehensive index.

ESSENTIAL **DK** COMPUTERS

I N T E R N E T

BUILDING A WEBSITE

T I M   W O R S L E Y

A Dorling Kindersley Book

Dorling Kindersley
LONDON, NEW YORK, DELHI, SYDNEY

Produced for Dorling Kindersley Limited by
Design Revolution, Queens Park Villa,
30 West Drive, Brighton, East Sussex BN2 2GE

EDITORIAL DIRECTOR Ian Whitelaw
SENIOR DESIGNER Andy Ashdown
EDITOR John Watson
DESIGNER Andrew Easton

MANAGING EDITOR Sharon Lucas
SENIOR MANAGING ART EDITOR Derek Coombes
DTP DESIGNER Sonia Charbonnier
PRODUCTION CONTROLLER Wendy Penn

First American Edition, 2000

4 6 8 10 9 7 5 3

Published in the United States by Dorling Kindersley Publishing, Inc.
95 Madison Avenue, New York, New York, 10016

A catalog record is available from the Library of Congress.

ISBN 0-7894-5526-9

Color reproduced by First Impressions, London
Printed in Italy by Graphicom

For our complete
catalog visit
www.dk.com

CONTENTS

THE WORLD WIDE WEB

The World Wide Web, commonly known as "the Web," is the largest and fastest growing area of the Internet. This chapter tells you what you can do on the Web and how it works.

WHAT IS THE WEB?

The World Wide Web is a vast information resource that exists around the world on hundreds of thousands of computers called Web servers. These contain websites that can vary in content from a single page to many thousands of pages that are electronically linked to each other. The total number of pages now available on the World Wide Web is numbered in billions. These pages add up to a global library of information that you can access and navigate by using your computer.

HOW THE WEB WORKS

The World Wide Web consists of countless pages all connected via the global communications network provided by the Internet. The connections between pages are made by hypertext links, or "hyperlinks," which are addresses embedded in the Web pages. These links may connect to pages on the same website, or to pages that are on a computer on the other side of the planet.

Your PC
You access the Web from your PC via a modem and an Internet Service Provider.

Web browser
You request Web pages from Web servers by typing a unique address into a program called a Web browser.

Modem
Modems enable computers to communicate with each other over the telephone network.

HOW DO YOU ACCESS THE WEB?

To access the Web you need a personal computer connected to a modem – an electronic device that translates the computer's digital signals into the analog signals that can pass along telephone lines. You also need an account with an Internet service provider (ISP). ISPs are your gateway to the Web as they operate powerful computers that are permanently connected to the Internet. Through your modem and your ISP, you can explore what is available on the Web by using a program called a Web browser.

Telephone line
The Internet uses existing telephone networks to carry information between computers located all over the globe.

• Satellite
Satellites can form part of the Internet network.

Service provider
Your ISP translates the Web address and sends your request to the correct Web server on the Internet.

Web server •
A Web server is a large computer that stores Web pages and makes them available over the Internet. It receives your request and sends the data for the relevant Web page back to your PC.

ISN'T THE WEB THE SAME AS THE INTERNET?

Many people use the terms "World Wide Web" and "Internet" to mean the same thing, but they are different. The Internet is a global network of interconnected computers that communicate with each other via the existing telecommunications networks. The Web uses the Internet network to access and link websites. As well as providing the infrastructure over which the World Wide Web is able to operate, the Internet offers a variety of other forms of communications and resources, including email, newsgroups, and discussion groups. If the Internet is like a system of roads linking places together, then requests for Web pages, and the data from Web pages, are just two of the many kinds of traffic that travel on this road system.

WHAT'S ON THE WEB?

The pages of the World Wide Web offer information on just about every topic you care to think of. Whether your interests include current affairs, astrophysics, golf, or Antarctic flora and fauna, somewhere there is certain to be a website devoted to that topic. The Web has always been the home of academic information, but in recent years it has also become an information base for public sector bodies, government departments and, most noticeably, commercial organisations.

Nonprofit organisations
Most major charities and non-profit organisations promote their work on the Web.

Education
Many leading universities and independent bodies offer courses that can be taken over the Web.

News
Broadcast corporations provide up-to-the-minute news of global events on the Web, often before it goes out over the airwaves.

Online games
You can pit your wits against opponents all round the world with online games.

Commercial organisations
You can buy anything over the Web, from books and clothes to your weekly groceries.

Research
Libraries, universities, public and commercial bodies, and individuals all publish information on the Web.

Government bodies
To email the President or contact your local council, you will almost certainly find the right address on a website.

Hobbyists
Individuals create their own websites on topics they are interested in, but amateur information is not always reliable.

WHAT'S ON A WEB PAGE?

When the Web started, Web pages contained only text and very basic formatting, and they offered very little in the way of design. Today's Web pages are a world away from those early pioneers and many sites now aspire to be multimedia extravaganzas. A Web page is likely to incorporate sophisticated graphics and include video clips, sound sequences, and interactive animations. You may even be able to play miniature software programs known as "applets" on the page.

Download files
Web pages can contain files that you transfer to your own computer to view or install.

Programs
While you are viewing a site, a program can run independently within the Web page.

Graphics
A well-designed website can be a showcase for the skills of the graphic designer.

Hypertext links
Use hypertext links, or "hyperlinks" to go directly to other relevant sites.

Text
Text within a page can be copied, pasted, and saved to your hard disk.

Multimedia files
These can be sound, video, or interactive animations.

Photographs
Images on a Web page can also act as hyperlinks.

HOW A WEB PAGE WORKS

Web pages are built using a computer language called HyperText Markup Language (HTML). HTML comprises a set of tags that identify the elements on a Web page as being of a certain type – for example, text, image, or multimedia file. The HTML tags tell the Web browser where to find the files needed to build the page, how to display them, and acts as the glue that binds them together on the page.

Browser window
This is how the Web page appears in the browser window.•

The <HTML> tag
This line tells the browser that the file is a HyperText Markup document.•

HTML code
This code tells the browser how to display a Web page. HTML instructions are known as "tags." View the code of a page by choosing "View Source" in your Web browser.•

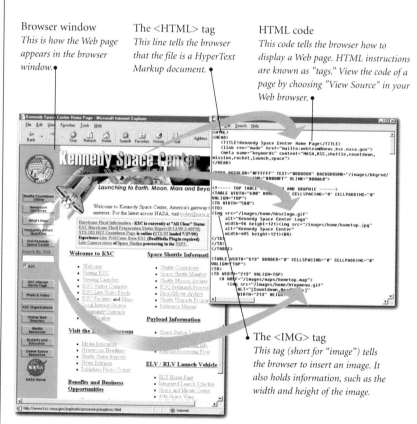

• **The <IMG> tag**
This tag (short for "image") tells the browser to insert an image. It also holds information, such as the width and height of the image.

WHAT IS A WEB BROWSER?

A Web browser is a piece of software installed on your PC that lets you look at (or "browse") different websites. The most widely used Web browsers are Netscape Navigator and Microsoft Internet Explorer. Navigator was the first to arrive and quickly became the most popular browser on the market. Microsoft then created its own browser, called Internet Explorer, and ever since there has been a strong rivalry between the two, but both are excellent browsers. You can have both of them installed on your PC, and which one you use is a matter of personal preference.

WHICH BROWSER?

The examples shown in this book use Internet Explorer, but the pages should look almost the same using Netscape Navigator. New versions of these browsers are released from time to time. For example, Internet Explorer 5 replaced version 4, adding new features. It is best to use the most recent release of either browser providing your PC has sufficient memory and speed to support it.

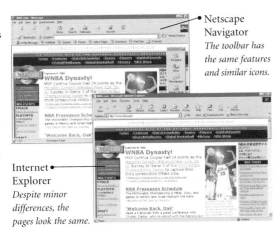

Netscape Navigator
The toolbar has the same features and similar icons.

Internet Explorer
Despite minor differences, the pages look the same.

MORE ABOUT BROWSERS

Most websites look much the same regardless of which browser you use. However, sometimes you might notice some small differences if you use both. This is because HTML describes how a page should look, and different browsers may sometimes interpret these instructions differently. Also, both Netscape Navigator and Internet Explorer support some tags that are "proprietary" – unofficial features of HTML that were designed to give users a reason to use that browser rather than the competition's. But these features are not widely used – most websites stick to using "official" HTML so that all browsers can read the page correctly.

MICROSOFT FRONTPAGE

FrontPage 2000 is a comprehensive website creation and management tool. Its flexibility makes it ideal for creating websites from personal home pages to corporate Internet sites.

WHAT CAN FRONTPAGE DO?

Creating the pages that make up a website used to be the exclusive preserve of computer programmers with a comprehensive knowledge of the HTML programming language, which is used to create Web pages. With FrontPage 2000, it is no longer necessary to know HTML. FrontPage 2000 carries out the programming for you in the background, allowing you to concentrate on the essential features in your Web pages such as design, feel, and functionality. The program is easy to learn and use because as well as containing advanced authoring tools, it also contains simple controls that you can begin to use almost immediately. FrontPage 2000 takes you through every aspect of creating Web pages from opening a blank screen to finally publishing your site on the Web.

WHAT IS FRONTPAGE?

FrontPage 2000 is essentially an editing tool, just like a word-processing program such as Microsoft Word. Whereas Word is used to create text and graphics that are eventually printed out on hard copy, FrontPage 2000 allows you to produce text and graphics easily and creatively, which will eventually appear on the World Wide Web.

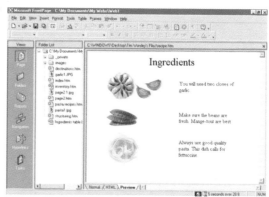

LAUNCHING FRONTPAGE

FrontPage 2000 is a powerful program that is probably different from any other kind of software that you've used.

However, FrontPage has many familiar features, and can be launched from the desktop just like any other program.

1 LAUNCHING FRONTPAGE VIA THE START MENU

• Place the mouse cursor over the Start button in the Taskbar and click. Move the cursor up the menu to Programs. A submenu appears on screen.
• Move the cursor across to Microsoft FrontPage and click the left mouse button.
• The FrontPage window opens on screen .

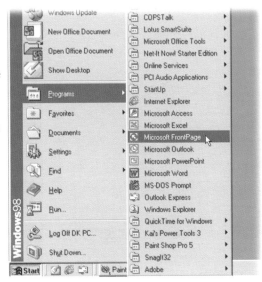

2 LAUNCHING FRONTPAGE VIA A SHORTCUT

• You may already have a shortcut to FrontPage on your desktop. Double-click the icon.
• The FrontPage window opens on screen .

THE FRONTPAGE WINDOW

The window that opens when you launch FrontPage 2000 has a style and layout that will be familiar to you if you've used other Microsoft Office 2000 applications. The features present in the window are designed around the actions that you carry out to create a website, and several view options to see what you've created.

THE FRONTPAGE WINDOW

1 The Views bar
To select the view options
2 Title bar
3 Menu bar
All the options in menus
4 Standard toolbar
Buttons for frequent actions
5 View title bar
Title of what is viewed
6 Workspace area
Where the Web is built
7 Formatting toolbar
Options for style and layout
8 Close view button
Closes the contents of display
9 Insertion point
Shows where typing appears
10 Page view
To view current Web page
11 Folders view
To organize files and folders
12 Reports view
Shows status of files/links
13 Navigation view
Shows navigation structure
14 Hyperlinks view
Displays Web's hyperlinks

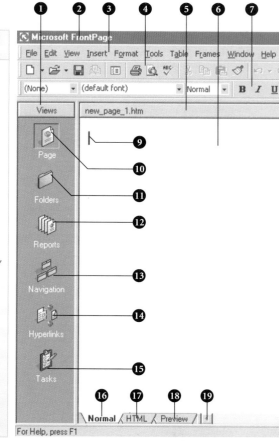

SMALL ICONS?

The Views bar is shown by default to the left of the workspace and allows you quickly to switch between views. If you prefer, you can use small icons in the Views bar by right-clicking on the bar and selecting Small Icons from the menu that opens.

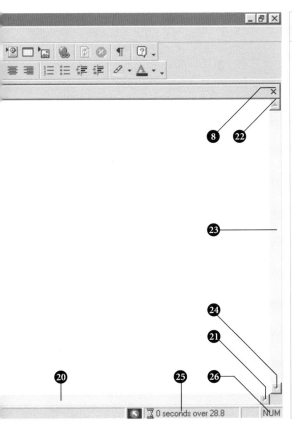

THE FRONTPAGE WINDOW

15 Tasks view
Shows outstanding tasks
16 Normal view tab
Web page is created here
17 HTML code tab
HTML code is shown here
18 Preview tab
Shows page in browser view
19 Scroll left arrow
Shows left side of page
20 Scroll bar
Used to move across page
21 Scroll right arrow
Shows right side of page
22 Scroll up arrow
Shows top of page
23 Vertical scroll bar
Used to show all the page
24 Scroll down arrow
To show end of page
25 Download time
Time taken for page to download
26 NUM lock
Shows that numeric keypad at right of keyboard is on

| 20 | Creating a Page |

| 30 | A word about download times |

THE FRONTPAGE TOOLBARS

FrontPage is part of the suite of programs that comprise the Microsoft Office 2000 suite. And as such its toolbars follow closely the style and layout of the other programs in the suite. You will notice a strong similarity to the toolbars that are part of Word because both Word and FrontPage feature powerful editing tools. Other toolbars are available for display in the FrontPage window, and if you want to customize these, follow the sequence of steps described opposite.

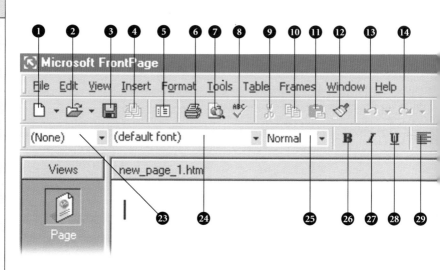

THE FRONTPAGE TOOLBARS

1 New page	9 Cut	17 Insert picture from file
2 Open file/folder	10 Copy	18 Hyperlink
3 Save	11 Paste	19 Refresh screen
4 Publish website	12 Format painter	20 Stop link or loading
5 Folder list	13 Undo action(s)	21 Show formatting marks
6 Print	14 Redo action(s)	22 Help
7 Preview in browser	15 Insert component	23 Style selector
8 Spelling checker	16 Insert table	24 Font selector

CUSTOMIZING A TOOLBAR

You can select which toolbars to see and their contents. Click Tools in the Menu bar and select Customize. The Customize dialog box opens. Click on the

Toolbars tab to see the list of ten available toolbars.

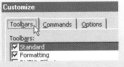

ScreenTips

You don't have to memorize what each button does. Just roll the mouse cursor over a button, wait one second, and a box appears and gives the button's name.

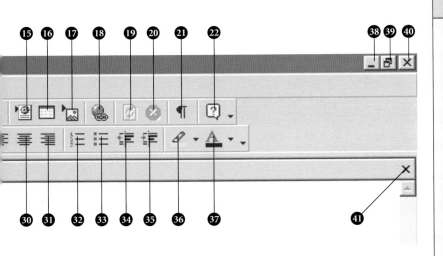

THE FRONTPAGE TOOLBARS

25 Font size selector
26 Bold
27 Italic
28 Underline
29 Align left
30 Center
31 Align right
32 Numbering list

33 Bulleted list
34 Decrease indent
35 Increase indent
36 Highlight color
37 Text color
38 Minimize window
39 Restore window
40 Close FrontPage

41 Close Web page

| 25 | Aligning text | 27 | Using Lists |

CREATING A NEW WEB

FrontPage removes all the hard labor from creating a new web.
There's no need to learn a new programming language because
FrontPage does all the programming for you in the background.

CREATING A FRONTPAGE WEB

FrontPage uses the concept of a "FrontPage Web" to organize the different files you create. This means you keep all the different elements of your website together in a group, which FrontPage calls a "web." Try to think of each FrontPage Web as a unique project that can be worked on as a whole, rather than a series of individual files. You will use FrontPage to create your FrontPage Web, which you can publish in its entirety. You can also make changes at any time and FrontPage will automatically update the rest of your site, keeping your site intact and error-free.

1 MAKING A NEW WEB

● To create a new FrontPage Web, launch FrontPage, click on File in the menu bar, and choose New>Web from the menu (i.e. choose New and then choose Web).

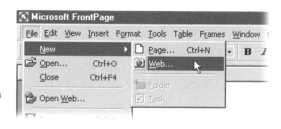

OTHER TYPES OF WEBSITES

FrontPage offers a variety of website types to choose from when creating a new Web. We have chosen a One Page Web, but the other Webs are fun to try out too. For example, choosing the Corporate Presence Wizard from the New dialog box launches a series of questions about you and your company, and creates the site structure based on your answers. You can customize the pages that have been created, and quickly have a good-looking website.

2 CHOOSING A WEB TYPE

● You are presented with the New dialog box offering a variety of different Webs. For now, just highlight One Page Web. You also type in a location where the Web is to be saved. In this example, the chosen path is: C:\My Documents\ My Webs\Web1, where "Web1" is the name given to the new Web if this is the first web that has been created. Click on OK when you have entered these details.

● A new Web is created containing an empty "home page" ready for you to customize, (a home page is the first page you arrive at when you visit a site).

The different types of Web on offer

Type the desired location of the new Web in this box ●

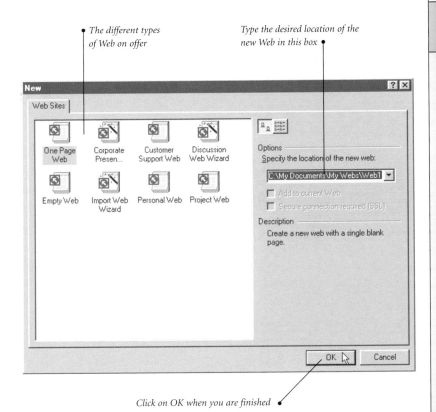

Click on OK when you are finished ●

CREATING A PAGE

So far you have created a One Page Web containing a single home page. This page is empty and is ready for you to start filling it with information, but before doing that it's important to know how to save the page and how to create new pages. You can see a list of the files in your Web by using the Folder List area of the FrontPage environment (if you can't see it, choose Folder List from the View menu). The Folder List area is similar to the Windows Explorer feature of Windows. The two folders, "_private" and "images" are created by FrontPage.

1 OPENING A PAGE

• Double-click on the file you want to open in the Folder List. In this case, double-click on index.htm (the default name of the home page).

• The page opens in Normal view in the main workspace area of the screen. Now position the cursor at the top of the page and type **Welcome to my home page!**

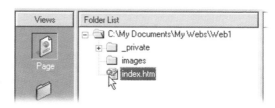

2 SAVING A PAGE

• Now that you have added some text to the page, you can save the changes you have made. Choose Save from the File menu (or click on the Save button on the Standard toolbar). The file is now saved.

Save button •

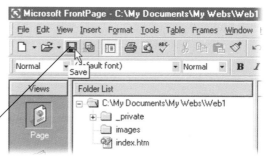

3 ADDING A PAGE

• To add new pages to your Web, pull down the File menu and select New> Page. A dialog box appears containing different types of pages. Just choose Normal Page and click OK.

• You can now add to this new page to your Web, just as you did with the home page. When you decide to save this page, the Save As dialog box appears.

• Type page2.htm in the File name: box and then click the Save button. The page is now added to your Web. You can add as many pages to your Web as you want whenever you want.

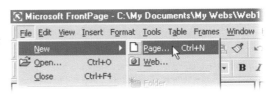

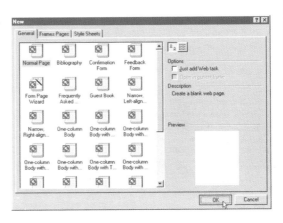

Enter a file name here •

Save button •

NAMING WEB PAGES

When choosing file names for your Web pages, there are some points to keep in mind. Avoid putting spaces in the name, as this can cause problems on some Web servers. Use the underscore symbol instead of a space, such as "new_page.htm." Some Web servers prefer all file names to be in lower-case letters, so it is common practice to use all lower-case file names as well. File names can be changed at any time.

PAGE PROPERTIES

A Web page has a set of "Page Properties," such as a title or a background color. When FrontPage creates a new page it gives the page a set of default properties, but you can easily change these properties to suit your individual taste. Every Web page should have a meaningful title because the title appears at the top of the Web browser's window on a user's screen when they visit your website. You can also alter the color of the background of the page, and change the color of different parts of the text.

1 ACCESSING THE PAGE PROPERTIES
● Right-click on an empty section of your page and, from the pop-up menu that appears, choose Page Properties by left-clicking on it.

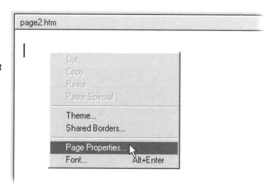

2 CHANGING THE PAGE TITLE
● Type a new title for your page in the Title box.

The Title box ●

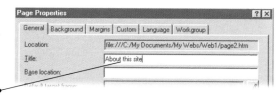

3 CHANGING THE BACKGROUND COLOR
● Click on the Background tab of the Page Properties dialog box.

• Click on the arrow to the right of the Background color box to view the background colors.
• Click on the drop-down color palette to change your page's background color.

Background color drop-down palette

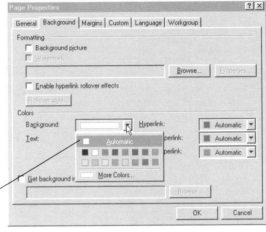

4 MORE COLORS

• If you need more colors than those on the initial palette, click on More Colors. Now choose from the wider selection.

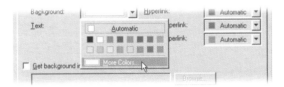

Click on a color to select it, and then click on OK

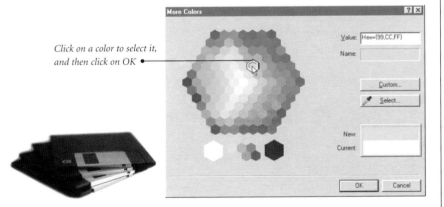

WORKING WITH TEXT

Text makes up the bulk of most websites. Learning how to create attractive text can make your website much easier to read and more enjoyable for your visitors.

ENTERING AND ALIGNING TEXT

Entering and aligning text using FrontPage is very similar to using a word processor, such as Microsoft Word. Text editing by using FrontPage should therefore be familiar to many people. The difference is that the text you type is formatted using HTML, which has a more limited range of styles than most word processors. However, you can still use most of the common techniques for text formatting, such as changing the alignment, creating headings, making text bold or underlined, and using different fonts and font sizes. Open the page called index.htm and begin the following exercises to build up your proficiency.

1 ENTERING TEXT

• As you have already seen, entering text into a Web page is easy. Simply click on the text area of index.htm and type in your text.

Help

index.htm

Welcome to my home page!

This is some practice text that I'm typing in to see ho manipulate text using Microsoft FrontPage 2000. N to press the Return key to start a new paragraph.

Here's my third paragraph.

2 ALIGNING TEXT

- Text can be aligned left, center, or right.
- To align some text, first highlight the paragraph you want to align, and then click on one of the alignment buttons on the formatting toolbar.
- To follow this example, highlight the paragraph "Welcome to my home page!" Now click the Center alignment button to move the paragraph to the center of the page.

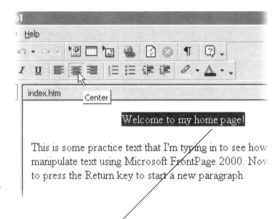

The paragraph is centered

STRUCTURING YOUR DOCUMENTS

HTML was designed to describe how a document is structured, and it contains a series of styles to help you do this. Each section of your document is given a tag that tells the browser what type of information is about to arrive. The most common tag is the paragraph tag. Each time you press Enter←┘ when typing, FrontPage inserts an HTML paragraph tag. There are also many other types of tags, particularly Header tags, which can help you to structure your text.

1 ENTERING TEXT

- Create a page called structuring.htm and type in some text.
- Highlight the first line and click on the Style selector box at the left end of the Formatting toolbar.

structuring.htm

About our company

Origins

We founded our company in 1998 with a staff of just
Although we started out small, we have grown as our
developed. We now have over 200 people working a

- Choose Heading 1 from the list of pre-existing styles. The line changes to a larger font.
- Now choose the second line and do the same except this time choose Heading 2.
- You'll see that the line changes to a slightly smaller font than the Heading 1 paragraph.
- Using the same method as before, make the fourth paragraph a Heading 2, and the fifth paragraph as Heading 3. Your page now has a logical structure.

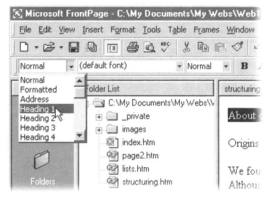

The first line now in the Heading 1 style

The second line now in the Heading 2 style

structuring.htm

About our company

Origins

We founded our company in 1998 with a staff of just t Although we started out small, we have grown as our developed. We now have over 200 people working a company headquarters.

THE BENEFITS OF STRUCTURING YOUR PAGE

There are good reasons to structure your pages by using different heading levels and paragraph types. For example, by defining one heading as a H1 header, and the next as a H2 header, a Web browser knows to display the first heading in a larger size than the second. The actual way the browser displays the heading (such as using a specific font size) is determined by the browser itself. One browser might use a different font size from another, but the important thing is that the browser knows the correct proportion, or structure, of the way you want your page to be displayed on screen.

USING LISTS

Many people like to use lists in their documents because they are easy to read and can help emphasize important information. Fortunately, HTML has a built-in list function, and creating lists in FrontPage is very simple. We will concentrate on the two most widely used type of list, the bullet point list and the numbered list. Follow the instructions below to see how it's done.

1 NUMBERED LISTS

● Create a new page and call it destinations.htm. Insert the cursor at the place where you want your list to start.

● Suppose you are a travel agency and want a list of your most popular holiday destinations. Type in a series of cities as shown in the example, pressing [Enter ←] after each city.

● Now highlight the series of cities and click on the Numbering button on the Formatting toolbar. FrontPage creates a numbered list and adjusts the line spacing.

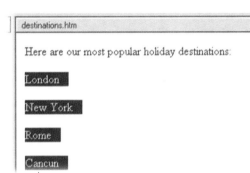

destinations.htm

Here are our most popular holiday destinations:

London

New York

Rome

Cancun

● *Type in a list of cities and highlight them*

destinations.htm

Here are our most popular holiday destinations:

1. London
2. New York
3. Rome
4. Cancun
5. Sydney

● *The Numbering button*

● *The list is now numbered*

2 BULLET POINT LISTS

• Next, create a list showing the different types of ticket on offer. Type in the list as shown in the example.

• As before, highlight the list and click on the Bullets button on the Formatting toolbar. FrontPage creates a bullet point list.

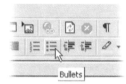

Bullets

We can offer flight tickets in the following classes:

First class

Business class

Economy class

We can offer flight tickets in the following classes:

• First class
• Business class
• Economy class

FONTS AND STYLING

When you simply type text into a Web page, you'll notice that it always appears in the same font. When a Web browser reads your page it will display it using its default font. However, a variety of fonts, sizes, and styles is available to you. The browser reads the font instructions contained in the HTML code and displays your page in the way you intended. This can help give your page a more professional appearance.

1 CHANGING A FONT

• Open the home page called index.htm and highlight "Welcome to my home page!"

• Click on the arrow to the right of the Font box to see the fonts on your PC.

• Select Arial.

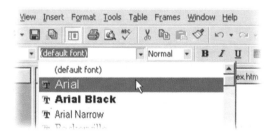

2 CHANGING THE FONT SIZE

• Next, click on the arrow next to the Font Size box on the Formatting toolbar to see a drop-down list of available font sizes.
• Choose 5 (18pt) from the list.
• The paragraph is now displayed in 18 point Arial, and stands out far better as a welcome to the page.

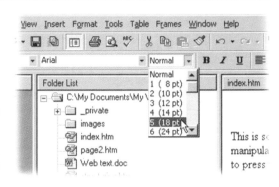

3 BOLD, ITALIC, AND UNDERLINE

• Using other text styles is easy. Just highlight a section of text (a word, a sentence, or a whole paragraph) and click on either the Bold, Italic, or Underline buttons.
• In this example, the word "third" is made bold.

The Bold button •

STICK TO A FEW COMMON FONTS

Using too many fonts can make a page look messy, so stick to using one or two fonts per page. Also, you might choose a font that a visitor to your website might not have. The Web browser substitutes the font with a close match, but the results are very unpredictable. It's best to stick to common fonts, such as Times New Roman, Arial, Helvetica, and Courier.

WORKING WITH IMAGES

Using images makes your Web come alive, whether they are pictures of products for sale, photographs on your personal page, or graphical menus and buttons to enhance your pages.

WEB IMAGE FILE FORMATS

In order for images to be used on a website they must be saved in the correct file format. The two most widely used file formats are the GIF (Graphics Interchange Format) and JPEG (Joint Photographic Experts Group) formats. These are the best formats to use because almost all Web browsers are able to display them. They are also useful because they are compressed file formats. This means that the image files are reduced in size when saved as a GIF or JPEG and visitors to your site are able to download the images faster. Without file compression, images take a long time before they are downloaded and displayed on screen. Potential visitors may decide that the wait is not worth it, and may leave your site.

A WORD ABOUT DOWNLOAD TIMES

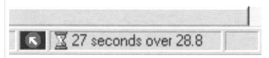

It's important to remember that adding multimedia files, such as pictures, animations, and videos, to a web page can increase its size very quickly and means that it will take longer for the page to appear when someone visits your site. This is because each image must be downloaded before it can be displayed on the page. The trick is to keep the overall download time for each page as small as you possibly can. FrontPage has a very useful feature that indicates the time it would take for each page to download using a typical 28.8K modem. This feature is displayed at the bottom right-hand corner of the FrontPage window. It's a good idea to keep this figure at less than 30 seconds. If you imagine doing nothing but waiting for over 30 seconds, you can understand how a site visitor might feel.

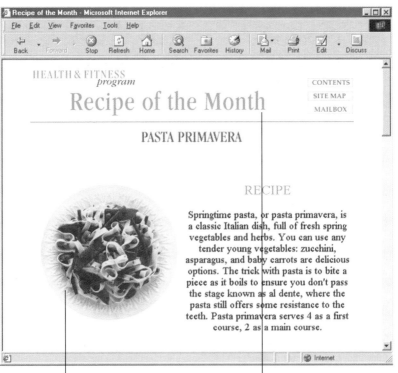

This is a JPEG image. It has been saved as a JPEG image because it is a photograph containing fine detail and many colors.

This is an example of a GIF image. It consists of high-quality type on a white background and is being used as a banner for the page.

JPEG OR GIF?

A basic rule of thumb is to use JPEG for photographs and GIF for almost everything else. The GIF image above consists of green lettering on a white background and is best saved as a GIF. But the pasta photograph is best saved as a JPEG. If in doubt, save the images in both formats and view them in a browser. Use the smaller file-size image if they appear the same.

INSERTING AN IMAGE

FrontPage's visual editing makes working with images very easy. But you need to acquire them from somewhere. A common way is to use a scanner to scan an image and save it on your PC. You can also save images directly from your browser when viewing other people's websites (although beware of copyright laws). Collections of images are available, usually on CD-ROM. And if you know how to create graphics, you can make your own images using graphics software.

1 SELECTING AN IMAGE

• Create a new page and save it as pasta pages.htm.
• Once you have an image saved as a GIF or JPEG, position the cursor at the place where you want the image to appear, and from the Insert menu choose Picture>From File.
• The Picture dialog box appears. Using the Look in: box, navigate to the location of your image.
• If you highlight the image you will see a preview of it in the window at right.
• Click on OK to insert the image onto the page.

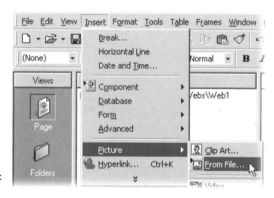

Image preview •

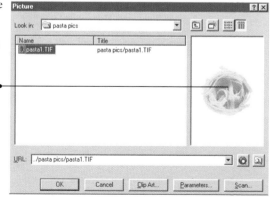

pasta pages.htm

The trick with pasta is to bite a piece as it boils to ensu
the stage known as al dente, where the pasta still offer
resistance to the teeth. Pasta primavera serves 4 as a f
as a main course.

The web image as it appears in the FrontPage workspace window ●

2 SAVING THE IMAGE

• When you save the page, FrontPage displays the Save Embedded Files dialog box, which asks if you want to save the image you have just inserted. Click on OK, and a copy of the image file is saved into your Web.

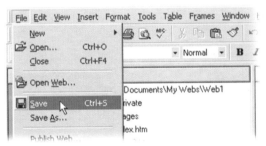

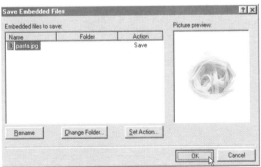

3 INSERTING CLIP ART

• FrontPage comes with a large selection of Clip Art for use in your website. Place the cursor where you want to position your clip art and from the Insert menu select Picture>Clip Art.

• Scroll down the icons in the Clip Art Gallery and click on Food & Dining.

• There are two clips available. Click on the basket of bread and click on the Insert clip icon.

• The clip is oversized, so right-click on it, select Picture Properties from the menu, and click on the Appearance tab in the Picture Properties dialog box. Click in the Specify size check box and enter 169 in the Width box – the Height box figure changes automatically to retain the proportions. Click on OK. The Preview screen can be used to show how the clip appears in your Web page.

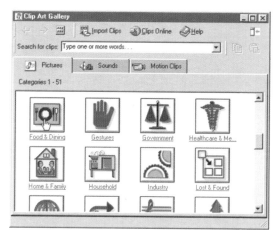

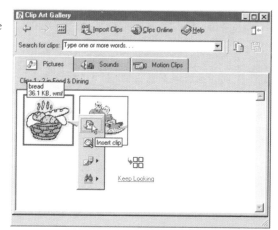

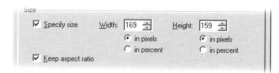

IMAGE PROPERTIES

Once you have placed an image on a page you can alter some of its properties, such as changing its alignment on the page, adding invisible space around the border, or giving it a textual name (known as "alternative text") that appears when you move your mouse over it in a Web browser. This last point is especially important as it can be an excellent aid to navigation, as well as being a useful description of what the image represents. It is also the text that will appear as the image downloads. This can be helpful to a visitor with a slow connection because it allows them to have some idea of what the image will be before it appears.

1 ALTERNATIVE TEXT

● First, open a page containing an image to which you want to apply alternative text (see above). Right-click on the image and choose Picture Properties from the pop-up menu that appears.

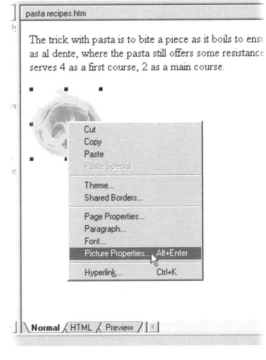

• The Picture Properties dialog box appears. In the section labeled Alternative representations, type **Pasta** into the Text box.

• When a visitor to your site waits for the page to download, "Pasta" will appear where the image is eventually positioned.

Low-res substitute

If you have a low-resolution image of the picture, you can enter its file name in the Low-Res box, and it will be displayed while the full image is downloading.

2 APPEARANCE OF THE IMAGE

• Now click on the Appearance tab in the Picture Properties dialog box. Perhaps you would like to make the image align to the right of the page. Click on the Alignment drop-down arrow and choose Right from the list.

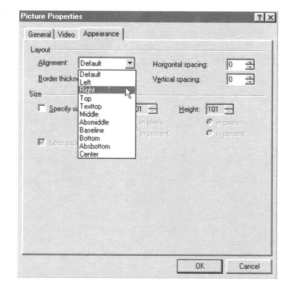

3 IMAGE SPACING

• You can put some invisible space around an image so that there is some space between it and any text that may be nearby.

• Again, in the Appearance tab in the Picture Properties dialog box, type 5 into both the Horizontal and Vertical spacing boxes. The units are pixels. Click on OK to save the changes you have made.

• The image moves across to the right-hand side of the page surrounded by the invisible space.

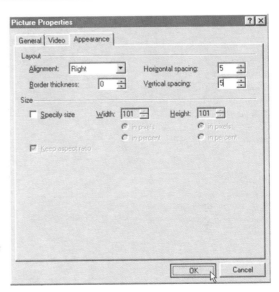

4 PREVIEWING THE IMAGE

• You can now see the results of your changes in the FrontPage workspace window. Try clicking the Preview tab and then moving your mouse over the image – the Alternative text appears.

Preview tab •

CREATING LINKS

A compelling feature of the World Wide Web is that you can link pages to create a "web" of information. The link could be to a page in your site, or to a site on the other side of the world.

CREATING A LINK

Creating hyperlinks between Web pages is one of the most fundamental skills you need when building a website. Without these links, a site would be nothing more than a collection of individual pages rather than a unified web of information. There are many types of link that you can make. You can link to another page in your site, or to someone else's site. You can create a link that sends an email, or you can place a link on an image. You can also make a link open in a new browser window. This section will show you how to master all these skills.

1 MAKING A TEXT LINK

● The simplest form of link is a text link. In this example we will make a link from the home page to the second page of the site.
● Open the home page, called index.htm, and type **Click here to go to the second page of my site.**

---

index.htm

Welcome to my home page

This is some practice text that I'm typing in to see how Microsoft FrontPage 2000. Now I'm going to press t new paragraph.

Here's my third paragraph.

Click here to go to the second page of my site.

2 SELECTING TEXT TO LINK

• Now highlight the words "Click here" and choose Hyperlink from the foot of the Insert menu. The Create Hyperlink dialog box opens on screen.

• The pages in your website are listed. We want to link to the file called "page2.htm" so click on that file. Its name appears in the URL box.

• Click on OK in order to create the link.

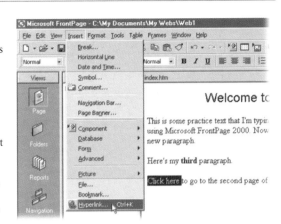

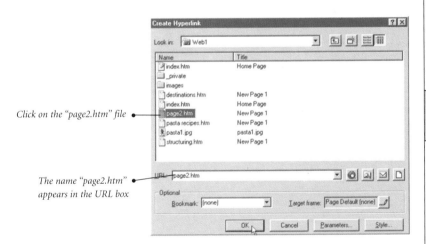

Click on the "page2.htm" file ●

The name "page2.htm" appears in the URL box ●

WHAT IS A URL?

URL means "Universal Resource Locator" – a Web page address. Most start with "http://", which tells the browser to use the HyperText Transfer Protocol – a communications protocol – followed by a Web address beginning "www." When you create a link, you are giving the browser a URL to link to.

3 TESTING THE LINK

• You will notice that the words "Click here" now change color and have a line underneath them. This shows that they are linked to another page. Change to Preview mode and try clicking on the link. It will take you to the file called "page2.htm".

index.htm

Welcome to my hor

This is some practice text that I'm typing in to see how using Microsoft FrontPage 2000. Now I'm going to p new paragraph.

Here's my **third** paragraph.

Click here to go to the second page of my site.

index.htm

Welcome to my homepage!

This is some practice text that I'm typing in to see how Microsoft FrontPage 2000. Now I'm going to press t new paragraph.

Here's my third paragraph.

Click here to go to the second page of my site.

Saving before linking
It is important to save your Web page before creating any links in it. If links are created before the Web page is saved, the links will not be updated if you change the location of your page.

Normal / HTML \ **Preview** /

4 CREATING AN EXTERNAL LINK

• Now let's make a link to another website. On the home page type **I made this site using FrontPage from Microsoft**.

• Now highlight the word Microsoft and click on Insert in the menu bar and choose Hyperlink.

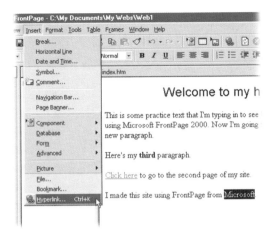

• This time, rather than choosing another page in your site, type: http://www.microsoft.com in the URL box and click on OK.

• This creates a link to the Microsoft website. You can make links to other sites in the same way by typing in different URLs.

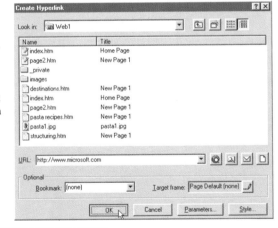

5 EMAIL LINKS

● Another useful link to make is an email link. When a visitor clicks on such a link, their email program launches and they can send an email to the address specified on your page. To make this kind of link, highlight some text as before and choose Hyperlink from the Insert menu again.

● This time, click on the button with the image of an envelope on it. You'll see the Create E-mail Hyperlink box appear. Here you should type in the email address to which you want to create a link. Then click on OK.

● The URL in the Create Hyperlink window changes and now begins with "mailto:" indicating an email link. Click on OK to create the new link.

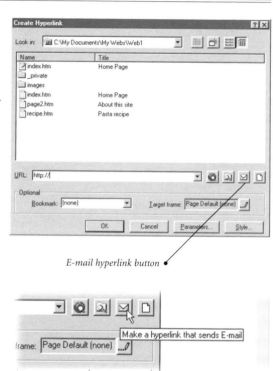

E-mail hyperlink button ●

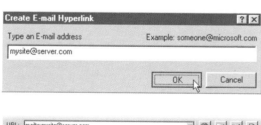

Recipient's email address ●

6 A LINK IN A NEW WINDOW

● Sometimes it can be useful to open a link in a new browser window. For example, you might want to send a visitor to another website, but also want to keep your own site open on their desktop. To do this, select some text or an image as before, but this time click on the pencil icon to the right of the Target frame in the Create Hyperlink dialog box.

● In the Target Frame dialog box, choose New Window from the Common targets list, and then click on OK.

● Now enter the URL of another website in the URL box and click on OK. When a visitor clicks on the link you have created, it will open in a new window in their browser.

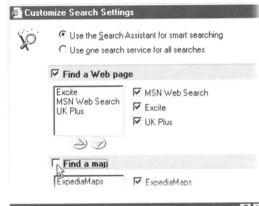

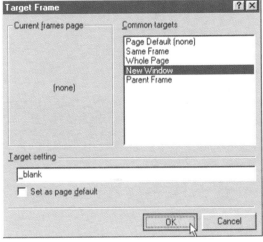

New page – new link
Clicking the New Page button to the right of the E-mail hyperlink button allows you to create a new page in your Web and to create a hyperlink to it.

USING TABLES

The use of tables in your website is a great way to present information in a clear and organized style. Tables can also be used to create more complex page layouts.

CREATING A TABLE

Creating tables in FrontPage is a very straightforward process. The most common use of tables is for laying out information in a style that is easy to read and understand. Let's take the example of an online business that sells guitars. They want to have a page on their website showing their current inventory, so that customers can quickly see what is available over their online system. This type of information is best presented in a table. As you will see, FrontPage gives you a great deal of control over how your table appears on your Web page.

1 INSERTING A TABLE

• First create a new page in your Web and call it "inventory.htm." At the top of the page type **Our Current Inventory** and press ⌐Enter←⌐.

• Now click on Table in the menu bar and choose Insert>Table. The Insert Table dialog box appears.

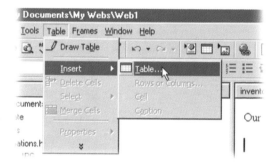

ROWS, COLUMNS, AND CELLS

Every table consists of table cells. Cells are the rectangular boxes in your table. A row is a horizontal series of table cells, and a column is a vertical series.

2 TABLE OPTIONS

● You can tell FrontPage how many rows and columns you want in your table. To create a table with 6 rows and 3 columns (you can add more later), enter these values into the Rows and Columns boxes.

● The Layout section contains options for greater control over how your table will look. First, specify the width by entering 400 and selecting In pixels – this means the table is 400 pixels wide (a pixel is a unit of measurement for computer displays).

● We want a border on the table. Enter 1 in the Border size box. Then click on OK.

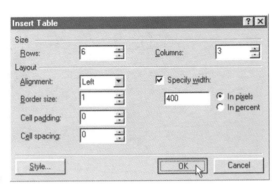

3 ENTERING DATA

● You can now start entering data. Either click in each table cell or press the ⎡Tab⎤ key to move to the next cell. The cell width alters according to the length of text that is entered. Fill in the table as shown in this example.

inventory.htm

Our Current Inventory

Make	Model	Quantity
Fender	Telecaster	10
Fender	Stratocaster	15
Gibson	Les Paul	6
Rickenbacker	4001	2
Gordon Smith	GS1	1

■ *A table cell* ●   *A row* ●   ■ *A column* ●

4 BACKGROUND COLOR

• One way to make a table stand out more is to use background colors. Highlight the first row of the table by dragging across it with the mouse.

• Now right-click on the row and then in the pop-up menu that appears, click on Cell Properties. The Cell Properties dialog box opens.

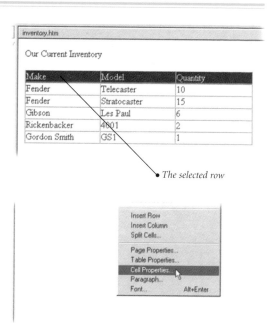

The selected row

Flowing text

If you want text to flow around a table that does not fill the width of the page, click on Table in the menu bar and select Properties>Table. Click on the arrow next to Float and select either left or right from the pull-down and click on OK. The table will move in that direction to make space for text, which will flow around it starting from the second row.

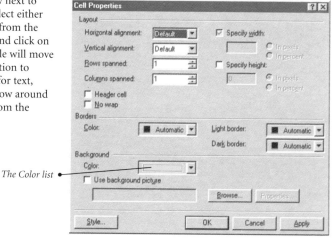

The Color list •

● Under the Background section select Yellow from the Color list and click OK. The background color of the row changes to yellow.

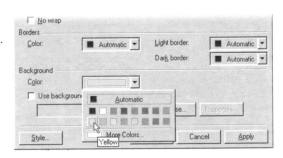

5 CELL PADDING AND SPACING

● The table is looking better, but the text is still quite close to the table's border lines. Change this by right-clicking anywhere in the table and choosing Table Properties in the pop-up menu.

● Enter a value of 2 in both the Cell padding and Cell spacing boxes. This inserts some extra space between the table entries, making them easier to read.

The Cell padding and Cell spacing boxes ●

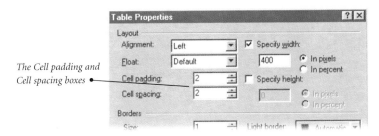

6 ALIGNING DATA

Each cell in the table is aligned to the left by default. However, perhaps you would like to align the Quantity column to the center. Highlight the entire column by dragging with the mouse from the top to the bottom of the column.

Now click on the Center button on the Formatting toolbar to change the alignment to the center.

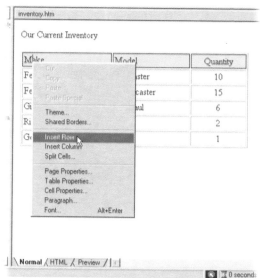

Drag down this column to select it.

7 ADDING A NEW ROW

The table would look better with a new row at the top containing a title. Position the cursor in the first cell of the table and right-click. Then choose Insert Row from the pop-up menu.

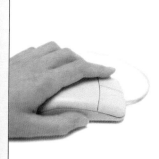

This inserts a new blank row of three cells above the top row of the table.

inventory.htm

Our Current Inventory

Make	Model	Quantity
Fender	Telecaster	10
Fender	Stratocaster	15
Gibson	Les Paul	6
Rickenbacker	4001	2
Gordon Smith	GS1	1

MERGING TABLE CELLS

Perhaps the new first row would look best as one long table cell. To merge the three cells together, highlight the entire row by dragging the mouse across the three cells.

Next, right-click in the row and choose Merge Cells from the list.

The three cells are now one. Type **Inventory** into the cell, and style the text as font Arial and bold.

Although you don't need to do it now, it's easy to split the cell into three cells again. Simply highlight the long cell, right-click in it, and choose Split Cells from the pop-up menu.

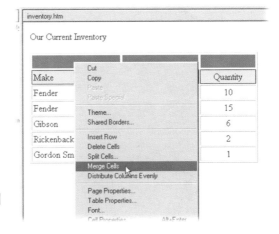

inventory.htm

Our Current Inventory

Make	Cut	Quantity
Fender	Copy	10
Fender	Paste	15
Gibson	Paste Special	6
Rickenback	Theme... / Shared Borders...	2
Gordon Sm	Insert Row / Delete Cells / Split Cells... / Merge Cells / Distribute Columns Evenly	1
	Page Properties... / Table Properties... / Font... / Cell Properties Alt+Enter	

inventory.htm

Our Current Inventory

Inventory		
Make	Model	Quantity
Fender	Telecaster	10
Fender	Stratocaster	15

USING TABLES FOR PAGE LAYOUT

Using tables with invisible borders around cells means that images and text can be placed with great accuracy. In the next example, a list of ingredients for a recipe has been created, but the same layout methods can be applied to your own images. First, create a new page in your web and save it as ingredients_table.htm.

1 CREATE A NEW TABLE

• Place the cursor at the top of the new page and from the Table menu choose Insert>Table .

• In the Insert Table dialog box, create a table with 4 rows and 5 columns. Specify the width as 500 pixels and make sure that the Border setting is 0.

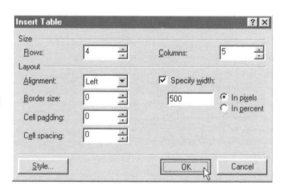

2 CHANGE THE COLUMN WIDTHS

• Although the border lines are invisible when viewed in a web browser, FrontPage displays them as thin lines as a design aid.

• Select the first column by dragging down it with the mouse so it is highlighted, and then right-click and choose Cell Properties from the pop-up menu.

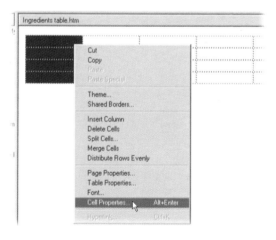

• In the Cell Properties dialog box click in the Specify width check box, then specify a width of 5 percent.

• Repeat this process for the third and fifth columns to produce the ingredients table as shown.

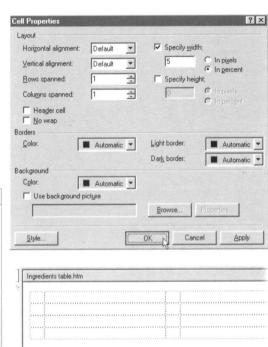

This is just one example of a table being used as a grid for laying out a page. There are countless variations, and the best way to learn is by experimentation. Try creating other layouts with different column widths and other combinations of rows and columns.

3 MERGE THE FIRST ROW

• Merge the first row of the table by highlighting it, right-clicking in it, and choosing Merge Cells.

• Next, type in a title for the page, highlight it, center it, and set it to font size 6.

INSERT IMAGES

Now you could put some images into some of the blank cells on the table. This is the same process as inserting an image on a page. Click in a cell and from the Insert menu choose Picture>From File. Navigate to the image you require and click on OK.

In the example, three images have been inserted into the cells that make up the second column.

ADD TEXT

You can now type in some text to accompany the images. Type the text into the empty cells in the fourth column as you can see here.

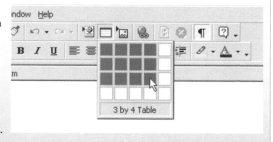

ALTERNATIVE TABLES

You can also insert tables by clicking the Tables icon in the Standard toolbar and dragging the cursor across the grid to select cells and columns. This method can also be used to insert a table within a table, for more complex layouts of images and text.

6 PREVIEW THE PAGE

• Click on the Preview tab to see how the page will look in the browser. Notice how the table border lines are no longer visible. The table structure we have created means that each element on the page is correctly positioned.

Preview tab ●

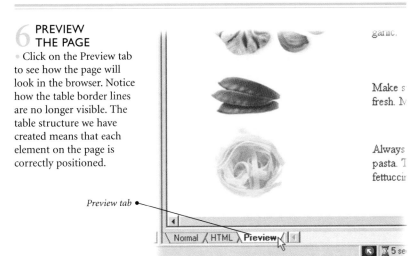

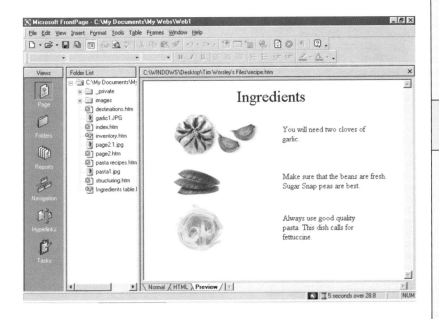

USING FORMS

Forms add an extra dimension to your website by letting your visitors send information back to you. This makes your website much more interactive, and potentially much more useful.

FORM ELEMENTS

A form consists of a series of labeled "fields" into which visitors can provide feedback. The form can then be submitted in various ways. For example, the information can be saved in a text file and analyzed later using a spreadsheet program. FrontPage makes creating forms very easy, allowing you to concentrate on the content of the form rather than on the computer code that allows the form to work. In these next pages you will see how to create a simple visitor-feedback form.

1 INSERTING A FORM

• Create a new page in your Web and name it "feedback.htm." Then type in some introductory text similar to the example shown here.

• Next, position the cursor beneath the text and from the Insert menu choose Form>Form.

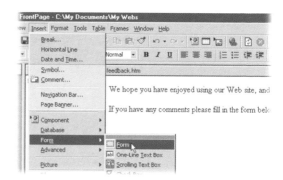

• A blank form is inserted, which contains a Submit button and a Reset button.

feedback.htm

We hope you have enjoyed using our Web site, and would love to hear from y

If you have any comments please fill in the form below.

[Submit] [Reset]

2 CREATE A FIELD LABEL

• Press Enter ⏎ twice to give you room above the buttons (note that the area of the form is marked by a dotted frame). At the top of the form, type **Name:** as a field label, followed by the Tab key to give some space.

feedback.htm

We hope you have enjoyed using our Web site, and would love to hear from y

If you have any comments please fill in the form below.

Name:

[Submit] [Reset]

3 ADD A TEXT BOX

• From the Insert menu choose Form>One-Line Text Box. A rectangular area will appear, which is where your visitor can type their name. Press Enter ⏎ to start a new line.
• Repeat the previous step so you have fields for E-mail, Telephone, and Fax.
• Use the Tab key to align each of the text boxes.

Microsoft FrontPage - C:\My Documents\My Webs

File Edit View Insert Format Tools Table Frames Window Help

Break...
Horizontal Line
Date and Time...
Symbol...
Comment...
Navigation Bar...
Page Banner...
Component
Database
Form
Advanced
Picture

Form
One-Line Text Box
Scrolling Text Box

feedback.htm

We hope you have enjoyed using our W

If you have any comments please fill in th

Name:

Name:

[Submit] [Reset]

4 A SCROLLING TEXT BOX

• Next you can insert an area where a visitor can write some comments. This is a different type of form field called a Scrolling Text Box.

• Type **Comments:** as a field label, press [Enter←], and from the Insert menu choose Form>Scrolling Text Box.

• You'll see a larger text box with scrollbars appear on the page.

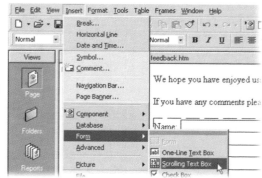

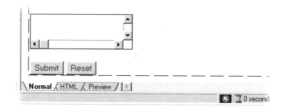

5 INSERTING RADIO BUTTONS

• Below the Comments box, type **Would you like to be added to our e-mail list?** You can now add two radio buttons to give your visitor a choice of Yes or No. From the Insert menu choose Form>Radio Button to insert the button.

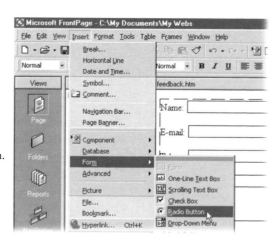

• Then type **Yes**. Press the [Tab] key, insert another radio button, and type **No**.

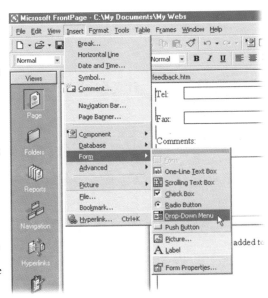

6 CHANGING A FIELD'S VALUE

• When the form is submitted, it will record which radio button the visitor clicked, but you need to give the button a meaningful name or "value."

• Double-click on the first radio button to access the Radio Button Properties dialog box.

• Type **OnList** in the Group Name box, and **Yes** in the Value box, followed by OK. Repeat the process for the "No" radio button. Still type **OnList** in the Group Name box, but this time type **No** in the Value box.

• Now, when the form is submitted, it records either "Yes" or "No" for the OnList field, making the results easier to read.

7 USING DROP-DOWN MENUS

• Under the radio buttons, type **Where did you hear about us?**, and then choose Form>Drop-Down Menu from the Insert menu.

• You'll see an arrow next to a small box, which is the drop-down menu.

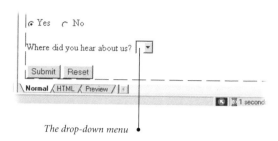

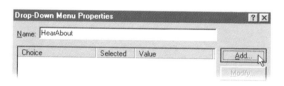

The drop-down menu •

8 ADDING TO THE MENU

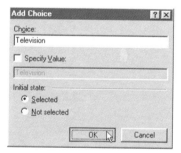

• You need to add items to the Drop-Down Menu. Double-click on it to open the Drop-Down Menu Properties dialog box.

• First, type **HearAbout** in the Name box (to name the menu), and then click on the Add button to see the Add Choice dialog box. This is where you can add items to the menu. Type in **Television** into the Choice box. Then click on Selected in the Initial State area. This will make Television the default choice when the visitor first sees the menu.

• Click OK, and then click on the Add button again to repeat the process to add Radio, Newspaper, and Other to the list of Choices. For these choices, choose Not Selected in the Initial State area – only one choice can be initially selected – in this case, Television.

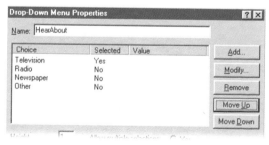

• Click on OK and save the page. You should now see "Television" as the first entry in the Drop-Down Menu. To see the menu properly, go to Preview mode and click on the arrow next to "Television".

9 STORING A FORM'S RESULTS

• You now have all the fields we require on the form – the final step is to tell FrontPage how to store the data when a visitor submits the form.

• Right-click anywhere on the form and choose Form Properties in the pop-up menu that appears.

• By default, FrontPage stores the results of the form in a text file called "form_results.txt" in the _private folder of your website (this is a special folder that can only be seen by you). Click on OK to accept this default.

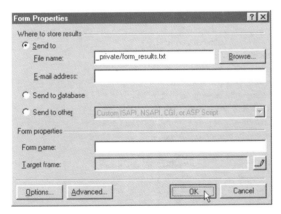

VIEWING THE RESULTS OF A FORM

To view the results of a form, open the _private folder and double-click on form_results.text. The file opens in a text editor and you will see each entry as one line of text with each field separated by a comma. This type of text file is a CSV (Comma Separated Values) file, and can easily be imported into most database or spreadsheet programs, such as Microsoft Access or Excel.

FRONTPAGE COMPONENTS

In addition to creating forms from scratch, FrontPage comes with a selection of prebuilt forms and other functions that you can easily use in your website. They require the FrontPage Server Extensions in order to work correctly, and are very simple to use. The two most popular components are the hit counter and the search form. The hit counter is a numerical display that records the number of times that a page has been requested by people browsing the Web, and the search form allows the visitors to your site to search it by using a keyword.

1 INSERTING A HIT COUNTER

• Open the home page of your site, and at the bottom of the page type **This page has been requested**, followed by a space. Now choose Component from the Insert menu, followed by Hit Counter. You'll see the Hit Counter Properties dialog box appear on the screen.

Here's my **third** paragraph.

Click here to go to the second page of my site.

I made this site using FrontPage from Microsoft.

Please e-mail me your comments.

This page has been requested |

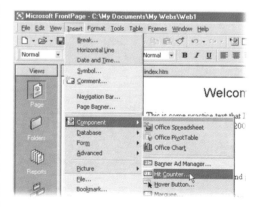

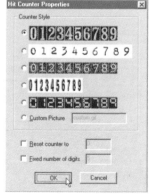

FrontPage Server Extensions
66

2 CHOOSE A STYLE

● You can choose a variety of graphical styles for the counter. You can also choose to reset the counter to a specific figure, and to limit the counter to a fixed number of digits. After you have made your selections, click on OK.

● When you look at your page, you'll see that FrontPage just displays a placeholder for the hit counter – this is because

I made this site using FrontPage from Microsoft

Please e-mail me your comments.

This page has been requested **[Hit Counter]** times.

the counter will only function after you have published the page to a Web server.

● Finish off the hit counter by adding a space after the placeholder and then

typing **times**. When the hit counter eventually becomes operational, it will now display a sentence that contains the total number of instances when the page has been requested.

3 USING A SEARCH PAGE

● You may have used search facilities that have been provided on pages in other websites. Here's how to create your own.

● Create a new page in your Web and name it "search.htm". This will be the page containing the search component. Add some introductory text at the top of the page – for example, **You can search our site by typing in a keyword into the Search box below:**.

● Now choose Component from the Insert menu, followed by Search Form. The Search Form Properties dialog box will now open.

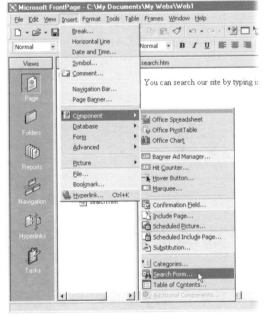

• You can customize the appearance of the search form by amending the values in this window. For example, to make the search box longer, type **30** into the "Width in characters" box.

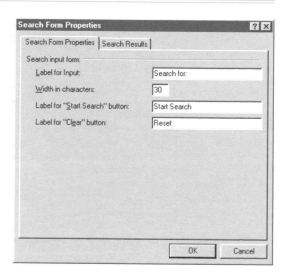

4 SEARCH RESULTS OPTIONS

• Next, click on the Search Results tab of the Search Form Properties dialog box. This is where you tell FrontPage how to display the results of the search. For example, for the most comprehensive results, tick the three check boxes under "Display options".

• When a visitor sees the results of their search, they see the file name, file size, file creation date, and a score (the higher the score the closer the match). Click OK to save your changes.

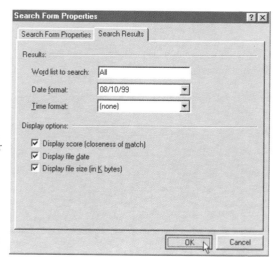

5 THE SEARCH FORM AT WORK

• The search form cannot work until it is published to a Web server. It will then appear in the browser window, and the visitor can type in a keyword, such as "pasta."

• After clicking on the "Start Search" button, the browser window refreshes itself and presents a list of results in a table below the search form.

• The visitor can then click on a document title to jump to that page.

The results of the search are displayed here •

You can search our site by typing in a keyword into the

Search for: |pasta

[Start Search] [Reset]

You can search our site by typing in a keyword into the

Search for: |pasta

[Start Search] [Reset]

Number of documents found: 2. Click on a docume search.

Search Results

Document Title	Date	Size	Score
Pasta Recipe	27 July 1999	1KB	316
Home Page	27 July 1999	2KB	156

PUBLISHING THE SITE

Once you have created a website you can check it for errors, and then make it accessible to others by using FrontPage to publish it onto the Internet.

CHECKING FOR BROKEN LINKS

One of the most frustrating experiences when browsing a website is to click on a hyperlink, only to find that the target page cannot be found. This is normally due to a broken link, which may have been typed incorrectly, or the page may have been renamed, moved, or deleted. FrontPage has built-in features to deal with the most common causes of links being broken, but there are times when broken links will still occur. FrontPage has a detailed Reports view that identifies broken links (in addition to other summaries) and has features to help you fix them. Begin by opening a page that contains links to other pages. In this case, the file, index.htm.

1 SWITCH TO REPORTS VIEW

● Click on View in the menu bar and select Reports>Site Summary. The Site Summary page opens containing detailed information about your site.

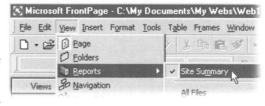

🏠 Recently added files	13	25KB	Files in the current Web that have been created in
🔗 Hyperlinks	8		All hyperlinks in the current Web
❓ Unverified hyperlin...	2		Hyperlinks pointing to unconfirmed target files
⛓ Broken hyperlinks	1		Hyperlinks pointing to unavailable target files
External hyperlinks	3		Hyperlinks pointing to files outside of the current W
Internal hyperlinks	5		Hyperlinks pointing to other files within the current \
⚠ Component errors	0		Files in the current Web with components reporting

Double click on this item to see the "Broken Hyperlinks" report

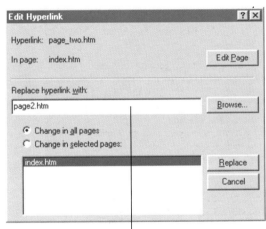

Broken Hyperlinks			
Status	Hyperlink	In Page	Page Title
Broken	page_two.htm	index.htm	Home Page
? Unknown	http://www.microsoft.com	index.htm	Home Page

2 FIND BROKEN LINKS

• Double-clicking on the Broken hyperlink line displays a detailed list. Earlier, a link was created to "page2.htm" (*see* p.39). Now we have deliberately created a broken link by renaming the link to read "page_two.htm".

• The first line of the list shows the broken link on the home page. Double-click on that line.

• In the Edit Hyperlink dialog box, type the correct name of the page in the Replace hyperlink with box. Click on Replace.

• The hyperlink is amended and you are returned to the Broken Hyperlinks report page. The corrected link is no longer listed.

• After working through other broken links in your site, the Broken Hyperlinks count on the Site Summary page should read 0.

Type the correct link in this box •

OTHER INFORMATION IN REPORTS VIEW

You will have noticed that there is a lot of other interesting information on the Site Summary report page, such as how many pages in your site would be slow to load, or how many pages have been recently added to the site. For most of the lines in the report, you can double-click on the line that interests you and see a more detailed report for that topic. Why not experiment and take a look at some of these other reports? They can be very helpful in analyzing your website.

PUBLISHING TO A WEB SERVER

When you are satisfied that your site contains no further errors, it's time to publish it to the Internet (sometimes called making the site "live"). However, before you do this, you must have somewhere to publish it to – in other words, you need access to a Web server. A Web server is typically a powerful computer with a high bandwidth connection to the Internet. It runs special software that handles requests for pages, runs scripts, and "serves up" Web pages. You may have access to a Web server via your company, in which case you can contact your technical support staff and obtain the details you'll need for publishing. Alternatively, you can purchase space on a commercial Web server.

1 FINDING A WEB SERVER

• Before you start, make sure you have all the necessary details about your Web server. You will need the URL of the server, and possibly a name as well as a password in order to gain access to the server.

• Make sure your computer is connected to the Internet and choose Publish Web from the File menu. Type the URL of your Web server in the box provided in the Publish Web dialog box. There is an imaginary name

in this example.
If you haven't already found a Web server on which to publish your site, you can click on the WPP's button. Doing so will take you to an area on Microsoft's website where you can find a suitable provider of Web server space (in FrontPage terminology, these are called Web Presence Providers). You can then sign up with one of these Providers and continue with the publishing of your site.

FRONTPAGE SERVER EXTENSIONS

The Web server you use should support the Front-Page Server Extensions. These Extensions allow you to use features such as the Hit Counter and the Search Form. They also allow the site to be admin-istered remotely and to be password protected. You can still publish your site without the Extensions, but you will not be able to take advantage of the features mentioned.

2 THE PUBLISHING PROCESS

• When you are ready, click Publish in order to start the publishing process. FrontPage will then attempt to connect to your targeted Web server.

• If you are asked for a name and password, enter these details when prompted. FrontPage will then start transferring (or "uploading") the files that make up your website. This may take a few minutes, depending on the size of

your site and the speed of your Internet connection. You will see a progress indicator showing how the publishing process is going.

• When all the files have been published you'll see

the window that is shown in the screen shot above .

• You can click on the "Click here to view your published web site" hyperlink to view your site in your Web browser.

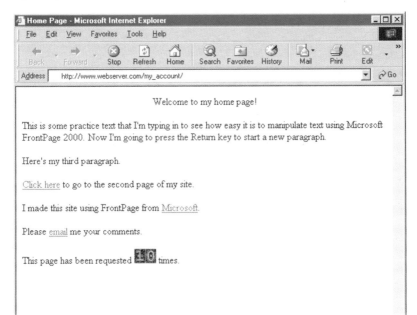

TESTING THE SITE IN A BROWSER

Congratulations! Your website should now be "live" on the Internet and available for visitors to browse. But before they do, it's a good idea to check the site yourself using a Web browser and make sure that everything is working as it should. Clearly the most important thing is to check that all the pages have been published successfully. You can do this by visiting each page in your site and checking that it loads into your browser window correctly. In doing so, you are also checking that each link is pointing to the right place. You can also check any forms or FrontPage components you have used, such as the Hit Counter or the Search Form.

1 ACCESSING YOUR SITE

• To check your website, connect to the Internet, launch a Web browser and type the address of the site into the Address box.

• Next, test the hyperlinks in your site by clicking on each link and making sure the target page loads correctly. In this example, click on "Click here" in the fourth paragraph and ensure that "page2.htm" appears on screen.

• Test any other links you have made in the same way.

If the link is working correctly page 2 should appear •

2 TEST THE HIT COUNTER

• Make sure the Hit Counter is working correctly by loading the home page and checking the Hit Counter paragraph. Click on Refresh in your browser window – the Counter display should increase by one digit.

This page has been requested **14** times.

This page has been requested **15** times.

3 TEST THE COMMENTS FORM

• Try filling out the Comments form you created earlier with some test information, such as your own name and details.
• Now click on the Submit button and make sure you see the FrontPage response screen with a review of the form's information.

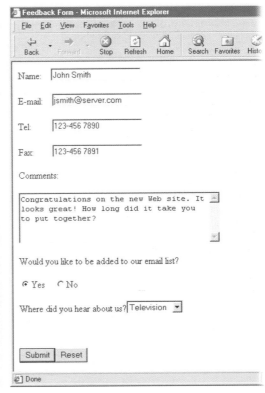

Spread the word...
After you have checked the site thoroughly give yourself a pat on the back – your site is now up and running! Remember to give out the URL of your site to friends and business contacts so they can see your work.

GLOSSARY

COMPRESSION
A system of reducing the size of a computer file, often to make the image faster to download.

DOWNLOAD
Transferring data from one computer to another. Your browser downloads HTML code and graphics to display a page.

EMAIL (ELECTRONIC MAIL)
The system of sending electronic messages between computers.

FRONTPAGE SERVER EXTENSIONS
Software that is added to a Web server to allow it to support FrontPage features such as components or remote administration.

GIF (GRAPHICS INTERCHANGE FORMAT)
A widely used file format for Web-based images.

HOMEPAGE
The first page you see when you arrive at a website, typically containing a welcome message and hyperlinks to other pages.

HTML (HYPERTEXT MARKUP LANGUAGE)
A computer language used to create Web pages. HTML consists of a number of tags that describe how a page should be displayed.

HYPERTEXT
A term used to refer to the technique of linking pages together with hyperlinks.

HYPERLINK
A shortcut to another Web page. You click on a hyperlink to jump to its target.

INTERNET
The network of interconnected computers that communicate using the TCP/IP protocol.

INTERNET SERVICE PROVIDER
A business that provides a connection to the Internet.

JPEG (JOINT PHOTO-GRAPHIC EXPERTS GROUP)
A file format for Web-based images, particularly for photographic images.

MODEM
A device used to connect to the Internet over a telephone line.

NETWORK
A collection of computers that are linked together.

NEWSGROUP
A discussion group on the Internet where people exchange news, views, and other kinds of information.

PATH
The address of a file on a computer system.

PIXEL
A unit of measurement for computer displays. A display consists of a series of pixels that display images on the screen.

PROTOCOL
A set of rules that determines how computers communicate with each other.

PUBLISH
You publish a website by sending its pages to a server.

SCANNER
A device that creates digital versions of images by scanning them with a beam of light.

TCP/IP (TRANSMISSION CONTROL PROTOCOL/ INTERNET PROTOCOL)
The protocol used by Internet computers to communicate.

URL (UNIVERSAL RESOURCE LOCATOR)
An address on the Internet. You type a URL into your browser to visit a website.

WEB BROWSER
Software used to view Web sites. Internet Explorer and Netscape Navigator are two browsers.

WEB PAGE
A single page on a website that can contain text, images, sound, video, and other elements.

WEB SERVER
A computer with a high-speed connection to the Internet that "serves up" Web pages.

WEBSITE
A collection of Web pages that are linked together in a "web."

WIZARD
A series of prompts to accomplish a specific task.

WORLD WIDE WEB
The term used to refer to all the websites on the Internet that are linked together to form a global "web" of information.

INDEX

ACKNOWLEDGMENTS

PUBLISHER'S ACKNOWLEDGMENTS
Dorling Kindersley would like to thank the following:
Paul Mattock of APM, Brighton, for commissioned photography.
Microsoft Corporation for permission to reproduce screens
from within Microsoft® FrontPage® 2000.
benjerry.com, CNN.com, wnba.com

Every effort has been made to trace the copyright holders.
The publisher apologizes for any unintentional omissions and would be pleased,
in such cases, to place an acknowledgment in future editions of this book.

Microsoft® and FrontPage® are registered trademarks of
Microsoft Corporation in the United States and/or other countries.

AUTHOR'S ACKNOWLEDGMENT
Tim Worsley would like to thank Julia
for her support during the writing of this book.